THE HEALING ROADS

Volume I

ASTA
PUBLICATIONS

"The Healing Roads Journal" Copyright © 2012 by Arteria Stevens

Library of Congress Cataloging-in Publication Data
Stevens, Arteria "The Healing Roads Journal"/ Arteria Stevens

Includes references and index

ISBN: 13: 978-1-934947-72-2

First Asta Publications, LLC trade paperback edition

1. Memoir-Non-Fiction. 2. Journal -Non-Fiction. 3. Child-Sexual Abuse Non-Fiction I. Title

Editor: Mary Jane Escobar-Collins
Proofreaders: Stephanie Sabeerin

Printed in the United States of America.

THE HEALING ROADS

Volume I

By
Arteria Stevens

HEALING ROADS

VOLUME ONE

For the most part, when people write their autobiography, it's because they feel they have something significant to share with others. There are lessons to be learned in life that many people miss. What makes our lives so significant on this earth is the fact that everything has a purpose. Things don't just happen. I looked back at all the painful memories in my past with the intention to search for the significant meanings behind those memories. I began to understand that there was a purpose behind every painful event in my life. I realized that everything painful and challenging in my life was designed to grow me, move me, change me, strengthen me, and make me wiser. This realization turned every tragedy in my life into a triumph. I discovered that life's journey is designed to be a victorious journey, in spite of everything. Being healed from severe depression, low self-esteem, the disease of pleasing people, marital and family problems, and the stigma of abuse and molestation are what compelled me to write about my life. Therefore, when I went back through all the significant memories in my life, I saw a lesson in every memory. Each lesson helped me to grow and mature to a new level in life, so I opened myself up and put all of those memories on paper, in order to be an example for others who may need encouragement in their lives. Molestation was just one of those circumstances in my life that helped me to grow throughout my journey in life. My book is about growing and healing through life's circumstances. As people mature in life, they can all look back and see that they come from a past. Everyone goes through pain at some point and time in their lives. In many cases, there is at least one traumatic situation in our lives that we can remember. Most of those painful conflicts get carried throughout our lives in an unresolved state and they become our issues. These very issues form our relationships. They affect the way we raise our children, the way we deal with our marriages, and the way we relate to others. In order to be in healthy relationships and have healthy attitudes about life, many of our past issues need to be resolved and healing needs to take place. I want to encourage everyone who reads my books; no matter what circumstances they have faced and are facing, to step out on their "Healing Roads." My book is also a celebration of my life. I can take the good, the bad, and the ugly, and celebrate everything in my life with triumph now that I understand there is a purpose for it all. Understanding the journey of my life gave me a purpose for telling it all. My greatest lesson was understanding that, "you can heal, you can move beyond 'unforgiveness,' you can become a better person, and you can live a better life."

At this time, I want to encourage you to begin your own journey towards healing. Your life, no matter how insignificant you look at it, carries a significant purpose; understanding that purpose is crucial to growing in life. Take some time to write about your early childhood. Think as far back as you can remember and begin to see how much history matters to you. Write about a very happy time and then write about an unhappy memory. After writing, reflect on your reaction to both memories just to help you to understand just how much of an effect your past has on you today. Think about how many other memories lying in your subconscious may be impacting your life today in ways you never realized.

∞

Take some time to write about a happy memory.

∞

∞

Now, write about an unhappy memory.

∞

How did you feel after writing about your happy memory?

_____

_____

_____

_____

_____

_____

_____

_____

_____

_____

_____

_____

∞

How did you feel after writing about your unhappy memory?

_____

_____

_____

_____

_____

_____

_____

_____

_____

_____

_____

∞

When it comes to unhappy memories, it's always good to talk about your feelings. Have you ever shared this memory with anyone?

_____

_____

_____

_____

_____

_____

_____

_____

_____

_____

_____

_____

∞

∞

When it comes to unhappy memories, it's always good to acknowledge and face the hurt. It doesn't matter how insignificant it may appear, pain is pain and all pain hurts. It doesn't have to be something as painful as what I have shared. All pain matters because you matter. It could be something as simple as a disapproving look, but if it hurt you then it is very significant and it is worth talking about.

Does the unhappy memory involve someone who hurt you?

_____

_____

_____

_____

_____

_____

_____

_____

_____

∞

∞

In order to begin the healing process, it's helpful to express your feelings whenever possible. Sometimes, however, it takes time and in many instances it may even take professional help before you are able to confront the person who hurt you. After quite a lengthy time of therapy, I was able to confront the person who harmed my daughter; even knowing they would deny what they did, but I confronted this person because the confrontation was for me and not for that person. I was able to confront my daughter's abuser calmly and without anger and I felt empowered when they lost control because I was able to stay calm. When you allow someone to make you angry and cause you to lose control, you give them your power and I knew I had nothing to feel guilty about. I knew I was telling the truth, so I felt really empowered to know that this person obviously was feeling guilty, while I had absolutely nothing to feel guilty about. I already knew and understood the statistics, which showed that most abusers never admit what they have done; however, I was determined to no longer live in fear of this person's denial over what they had done. Healthy confrontation is a necessary part of the process towards healing because it gives you back your power and releases that person's hold from fear of the confrontation that usually hangs over you; however, you have to make sure that you are healed enough to confront without losing control. Understanding psychological factors helped me to understand what and why I was confronting. For me, because I was able to confront in a healthy manner, I was able to also forgive and release this person to God, in spite of their denial. What they did to my daughter is no longer my problem, it is now between them and God. It's perfectly okay if you are not at a point where you can confront the person who may have hurt you, no matter what they did because sometimes it takes time and more healing first.

∞

Have you told this person how much this unhappy memory hurt you or how much what they did hurt you?

_____

_____

_____

_____

_____

_____

_____

_____

_____

_____

_____

_____

∞

Many times people carry hurtful scars into their adult lives without ever realizing the impact it has on how they handle life and relationships. Recognizing pain can help you to also recognize patterns of behaviors within yourself. It can also lead to a maturing process towards positive change. This process has helped me to become a better person. My number one goal in life is to work on continual improvement in my life and I will never stop working on myself. I embrace every painful memory I have ever held on to because I find so many inspiring lessons inside of life's painful moments. Life has a way of teaching you both what to do and what not to do, and I am a much wiser person having taken a deeper look at my life. That's how you turn the bad things that happen in your life into good things; by learning and growing from everything. It changes everything shameful or condemning into something tangible to help someone else. I ask God every day to show me what I need to learn in order to help me continue to grow and move forward in life instead of finding myself stuck all the time and not getting anywhere.

Do you still feel hurt or anger about the unhappy memory you wrote about?

_____

_____

_____

_____

_____

_____

_____

_____

_____

_____

_____

_____

∞

Acknowledgement of hurt and anger is actually a positive start towards the healing journey and it often takes courage to face pain. You can't change what you don't acknowledge, as I've said time and time again, so congratulations for stepping out onto your *Healing Road.*

∞

One day I took a seat, exhausted from working long hours at my office. As usual, I didn't find my life to be satisfying or complete. My mind was in its usual battle of confusion because I was trying to find answers to questions that I had. I gave up my work in private childcare seven years earlier in pursuit of what I thought would be an instant six figure success, running my own business as a financial analyst. I averaged sixteen to twenty thousand dollars a year in sporadic commission checks, yet I was convinced I could build a six figure income business. *"What I am doing is a financial ministry,"* I kept telling myself over and over. Families are so grateful for my help. I have a tremendous passion for helping people, but something was holding me back. Something kept putting me at a standstill; sometimes for weeks at a time. I had to ask myself, *"Why am I not as successful as many others in my business? Why am I not complete? Why does my life feel so unbalanced?"* I made a decision one day to sit still and figure out what was the missing element in my life. I took a deeper look and embarked on a spiritual and emotional journey I had never known before. I call it my "Healing Roads."

I discovered there was excessive baggage I held on to regarding my painful life of sexual abuse growing up. Fear was my enemy all these years. I realized, in order to dump the heavy loads I carried around with me, I had to allow myself to take a journey back through the history of my life. I didn't know how far I would be traveling, but I picked up my pen and paper and began to just write and write. As I wrote, I saw many things in my life that mattered to me. My life didn't just revolve around the pain of molestation, but the joy and pain of life itself. The easy part was reflecting on the joyful times. The difficult part of my journey was facing the pain. There were days I cried many tears while writing, but instead of running from the tears, I questioned the pain itself until I was satisfied with all the answers. Fear always hindered my course in life, unless I conquered it. I turned to my higher power and waited patiently for answers. Every answer that transcended throughout my mind seemed to indelibly

∞

fill the voids in my life. And so it continued; my "Healing Roads" journey of memories; some emulating heartfelt laughter and joy, others conjuring tension and pain as I relived being hurt throughout my childhood.

It was a necessary journey, for the purpose was to allow myself to learn lessons and grow. In the end, I now embrace my life and I understand that both the laughter and the pain are a necessary part of the process."The Process"; it's what life is made of and as you go through it, you'll find it's not so bad after all. The most integral part of my process is to become an open book of lessons. Three volumes later and I've succeeded at being vulnerable for the greater cause of being a living contribution to the world.

Now that you've written some things about your early years, go back and reflect on what you've written. Look at your life now. Think about your early childhood. *Are there some things that still bother you today?* Take some time to reflect on those things and write those reflections down. Question those moments in your life and search out things that you don't understand about those memories. Continue to ask yourself pivotal questions and see what answers are lurking inside of you, as I was able to see.

When I first began writing about my life, I was in a painful place in my life. I was confused, angry, sometimes blaming others, too afraid to confront, and sometimes too afraid to even acknowledge what I was feeling. Now, when I look at all that I have written I realize that I have changed my views on some of what I have written. Originally, I started going back and changing certain sentences where I expressed anger and pointed my finger at others. In the midst of trying to change some things, I suddenly halted. I realized that I needed to show myself in the painful stages of my life because so many people are still hurting and wounded and in search of validation. The journal that you are reading will show an imperfect person in the process

∞

of healing. Sometimes, I learn the right lessons and sometimes, especially in "Don't Touch Me" Volume I, I fall short of the lesson. As the journals progress, the lessons become more apparent to me. By the time you get to the end of Volume III of the book and the journal, you will find that I will have become both wiser and stronger. You will see that I have changed significantly.

This book is designed to take you on a journey of your very own. The more you read my journal, you will discover things that will draw you to want to write your own journal. Go to the first blank page at the back of this book and fill in your name on the top line and begin your own journal. You too will come our victorious.

I am proud of every reader for having the courage to heal.

∞

In chapter one of volume one, I wanted to understand why Granddaddy did this to me as I relived the memory of what happened. I sought after the answers by studying sexual abuse, in order to understand the perpetrators' mindset. I knew by now it wouldn't have done any good to rely on Granddaddy for any reasonable answers. He didn't understand why he molested me because he lived in a confused mind himself. Confronting him may have given me peace, but not answers. Confrontation is good because it releases the fear and the control that the person has over you. This fear is often in the part of your mind, which is occupied by the memories of what was done to you.

I discovered the definition that best described my granddaddy after I read and studied the characteristics of a pedophile. Once I understood, I realized that Granddaddy was a typical pedophile. Pedophiles are adults who engage in sexual activities through contact with children. Pedophiles assume children won't tell. They use friendship, love, and trust simply to deceive. With many pedophiles, their actions are not about sexual gratification, but about control or abuse. In their mind, many times they honestly believe they are showing love to the child they are molesting. They are so confused that they think what they are doing is perfectly alright. One problem with this thought is that they usually don't want anyone else to know about it.

Long before I ever started visiting Granddaddy, he had already fantasized about being with a child, as pedophiles do. He excused it as not being wrong in his mind a long time ago. He had already replaced the wrong feelings with every excuse he would allow his mind to imagine, in order to rid himself of any guilt or blame. All a pedophile needs, after they've fantasized and excused themselves of any wrong doing regarding their thoughts, is an opportunity to get a child alone. I just happened to come along. It was nothing I said or did. It was his delusional fantasies that caused him to molest me. It was not my weight gain or the fact I sat on his lap and allowed him to kiss me.

∞

How was I to know any better as a child? It is an adult's responsibility to display responsible and healthy behavior towards children.

I understand the emotional damage that abuse can cause. Some victims have had something similar to this and more happen to them. Being abused in any way creates a struggle with one's identity as an individual. It leads to low self esteem, depression and deeper issues for some victims. From this one incident, a part of me withdrew, and I lost my voice. I became afraid to speak up for myself. By the time I became an adult, I still didn't know how to speak up for myself. I understand the damage that people cause each other on a day to day basis, even with words, whether intentional or unintentional. The common bond between us all is the pain, shame, blame, and confusion we carry around. Going back to this memory has helped me to find my voice. If I can find my voice, I can find the me that's been lost for so long.

Write about another painful memory and then go back and re-read it to see if you can understand why that person or thing hurt you so much. Look for psychological factors in the library or on the internet. For instance, if it was verbal abuse, read books or stories dealing with verbal abuse or Google verbal abuse on the internet and see what you come up with that may help you to understand that person's motives. Write down everything you find out about what happened to you. I promise you that if you take the time to research and learn about things that may motivate specific abusive behaviors, it will help you, as well as someone else in gaining more understanding. I'm proud of you for having the courage to look at your pain.

∞

In chapter five of volume one entitled "Shon," my pattern was to protect my Daddy from going to jail. I had to make sure we stayed a happy family since Mama wasn't threatening to leave and take us away like she used to when we were small children. I was doing a good thing.

Yet again, I didn't have the proper definition or understanding of molestation. I just felt like it was inappropriate. During my research, I discovered that when an adult makes improper sexual advances, including asking me to sit on their laps, on their private parts; it's legally defined as an act of molestation. The charges that might have been brought against him depend on the state we lived in. Had he sat me on his bulge, it would have been considered sexually illegal if he was found guilty. I figured it would have boiled down to his word against mine. At this age I didn't think it would be considered a crime by law and it made me react differently as I tried to move on. Only, my subconscious wouldn't lie to me. My true feelings were totally locked away, but not gone. I planned to keep this locked away. What I didn't realize was that when you lock things away, you just end up carrying baggage around with you until you find it again. Every time I found the baggage again, I either tripped over it and fell down or mishandled it as I continually began to form a big "Don't Touch Me" stamp on my head. I'm certain I ran across this baggage many times in my lifetime; I just didn't recognize it. I didn't understand it began to form parts of my behavior and character. I'm glad I'm pulling out all my excess baggage, examining it and cleaning out the things I need to clean out.

In volume one, chapter seven entitled "Jan," I look back on this experience and I think about all the girls like me who have gone through their period of experimenting. I wonder how many of those girls were molested or abused, especially by the opposite sex. I went through a period of confusion for a time afterwards, wondering if girls were more tender and gentle towards you than guys because Granddaddy's bulge hurt me when he pressed against me. I feared

∞

other boys might hurt me as well. I wondered if it might be safer if I were involved with girls. By this time, I was starting to think boys might be too rough and hurtful.

My sexual experience with Jan could have very well turned me total ly off of the opposite sex and led to even more confusion due to the pain I carried from having been molested and the stigma I carried around regarding the opposite sex. The vast majority of males and females I've spoken candidly to, who consider themselves gay, have been molested, abused, disappointed or hurt in some way by either the same or the opposite sex. I've also learned every experience isn't necessarily unpleasant for every child who is sexually abused, which leads to even more confusion. I didn't have pleasant experiences with any of the adults who touched me over the years, but it's different depending on the assailant's intents and the state of mind of the child at the time of occurrence.

Whether or not a child enjoys the sexual experience, it is not the child's fault. I've heard a lot of young men talk about enjoying the sexual experiences at eight and nine years old while being molested by an adult. I've also met gay people who say they didn't have a molestation or abuse story to tell. I'm sure not every gay person has a story to tell relating to abuse. However, when I hear stories of abuse coming from a gay person, I don't see gay; I see confusion and mixed emotions being misdirected; I see pain that was not dealt with.

The adult in authority has the responsibility to act appropriately, not the child. A child can't seduce an adult who understands their proper role and responsibility to a child. Turning to the same sex as a result of abuse could possibly be a search for love. Sometimes, it's simply unexplained or misplaccd feelings. I believe some sexually abused victims begin to believe they were born gay. Most children never talk about their gay feelings with their parents or guardians, which leads to more confusion and misdirection over the span of childhood.

∞

In volume one, chapter ten entitled "Pastor," everybody wants to matter. In fact, I wanted to matter so much I thought about the possibility of saying something out of desperation to try and make up with my abuser, Pastor Jacobs; this is how much being important meant to me. Approval was more important than exposure. I didn't tell on Pastor Jacobs, because in my mind, I thought I would no longer be approved of for starting up what I believed would only be trouble if I told. My need to please people grew stronger. Pleasing people is a destructive addiction in which most people never understand.

In all actuality, Pastor Jacobs is considered a pedophile. I needed to understand the 'why'. After years of being damaged and confused, I knew I would need to understand the characteristics of a typical pedophile. Understanding the mindset of Pastor Jacobs and Granddaddy has helped me to resolve a lot of guilt and allow me to begin the healing process. I discovered that pedophiles genuinely like kids. Somewhere along the way their thinking regarding love, sex, and kids became completely mixed up. I also read that most pedophiles are very insecure and feel lonely. They feel only children will give them unconditional love and in their psychologically unbalanced minds, they equate love with sex, even when the object of their affection is a child. They don't view their behavior as wrong. I now realize pedophiles find ways to be around children as often as possible even though most people who work around children are not pedophiles. Pedophiles blend in with the mixture of morally upright people and are hard to weed out.

Because of my sexual trauma, I didn't have a healthy attitude regarding sex growing up. I found myself repulsed at the thought of any kind of sexual behavior involving touching my private areas or kissing with tongues. I envisioned a simple closed lip kiss as acceptable. I envisioned the thought of nakedness in front of a boy nauseating and degrading. I was hoping to find a good guy who wouldn't want to do any of these kinds of things with me.

∞

In the earlier part of chapter ten, before sharing my story about being molested by Pastor Jacobs, I shared my story about what happened on the day I started my menstrual cycle. As far as how Mama handled my menstrual cycle, I understand parenting doesn't come with a book. Children are raised by their parents and grow up and become parents as well. They end up following a lot of the same ways, traditions, and habits taught to them. Mama didn't understand the proper way to handle me starting menstruation. She was uncomfortable talking to me about sexual things, period. I was most likely just as naïve as she was about sexual matters growing up. This suggests that Mama may have unresolved childhood sexual trauma she hasn't confronted; even though I can never be sure unless she told me, which she hasn't. My lesson is to understand the shortfalls and do a better job with my child.

Nonetheless, Mama not knowing how to talk openly about my sexual maturity doesn't make her a bad parent. We all individually have shortfalls and areas that need improvement. Now, as an adult looking back, I'm taking an opportunity to look at my own shortfalls and working to improve upon them. I need to recognize that the different problems I carried over into my adult life were a result of being sexually abused. In my mind, this is not about Mama, but about using situations to help me to excel and be better. I'm happy for this memory as I look back with laughter.

∞

In volume one, chapter eleven entitled, "Crush," I felt that the only one I could really trust was me. I continued to be secretive and untrusting. I'm learning now to examine all of my secrets. I find an inappropriate behavior attached to every single secret I've ever had. I realize now that most secrets are indicative of shame. Even as an adult, I began to realize that many of the things I labeled as "my business," was usually something that wouldn't meet the approval of the ones I didn't want to know it. It didn't matter to me if the whole world knew about all the things I was proud of, and I never got angry if anyone talked about me in a good way. I only accused people of spreading my business if it was problematic or shameful. Now I can tell my stories without any inhibitions about exposing myself because I don't have anything to hide. I don't need approval. I need self-assurance in knowing who I am. I may have done what you say I did, but I'm not who you say I am; as often quoted by a Bishop who presides over one of the mega churches here in Georgia. I'm free now, so I can be a teacher by learning and sharing.

In the seventh grade, I thought what mattered was having someone in my life who I felt could see beyond sex. I thought every time Antonio stayed within certain boundaries, he was proving to be someone who finally liked me and not just my body. I wasn't thinking about age. I just wanted to feel loved by someone who treated me differently.

Why weren't my parents' love enough for me? I am realizing deep down inside, I felt I was loving my mama and daddy more than they were loving me, because I kept sacrificing my body every time I walked away from my abusers and kept silent. It went back to my granddaddy. Mama and Daddy seemed to care more for the welfare of the abuser. They didn't want Granddaddy to go to jail. It was more about him than it was about what he did to me. Deep in my subconscious, I didn't feel like Granddaddy paid for his wrong doing. I had

∞

to live with this and it affected me even though we never saw him for many years.

Something deep in my subconscious kept hinting that Mama and Daddy loved me, but only to an extent. Even though my carnal mind said, "But Mama and Daddy do love me though." And, of course they did. People, however, can only love you to the extent in which they are able to love themselves. *Did Mama and Daddy love themselves enough?*

For every one who is abused, I understand walking away from the situation doesn't change the situation, nor does it heal the situation. Thousands of victims just walk away from the situation and carry a lifetime of scars with them. The purpose is abandoned when you don't heal from the situation. You can't carry unhealed scars around with you. Scars unhealed become open wounds and then you end up with new wounds on top of the old scars. You have to confront your issues and you must confront your abuser. For some, it may take counseling or therapy to be able to confront your abuser in the proper manner. You have to be willing to forgive once you confront. There's also a time for releasing yourself from it all. Abuse doesn't have to dictate your life. You can turn it around and use it for good.

Now, what next? Where do I go from here? How do I heal? It would take a long time to figure this one out. Without understanding any of this at that time, my journey was just beginning. I still had lessons to learn.

$$\infty$$

In volume one, chapter twelve entitled "Tongue," here again, I was just a child in the seventh grade. I didn't understand the appropriate way to handle this situation. I didn't want Daddy to hurt anyone and go to jail. I knew beyond a shadow of a doubt that Daddy would have tried to harm Tongue had he found out what he did to me. In fact, I thought he might kill him, or at least attempt to. Tongue needed to be reported to the proper authorities for what he attempted with me. It was his mother, Ms. Pookie who didn't handle the information appropriately. She was the adult.

If my father ended up in jail, it would have been his choice, not my fault. My purpose was to be a voice for other potential victims who often fall in line right behind the first victim. Every time I kept silent, I left an open door for the person who needed to be stopped. I gave them the opportunity to keep on doing it to someone else. I'm not pointing this out to say this was my fault. My lesson isn't about fault or blame. My lesson has become a simple observation on how to handle a person who is sexually aggressive towards you, AGAINST YOUR WILL.

In order to understand why Tongue did what he did, I again researched to find particular clues that purveyed the mindset of a typical rapist. I discovered that rape is a sexual expression of power and anger. Over half of all sexual offenders admit to other acts beyond the one in which they have been convicted of, including battery, sexual assault, or attempted rape, or physical and sexual abuse of a child. As a child, if I could have learned to only control what I had the ability to control without blaming myself or making myself responsible for things beyond my control, then I would have made the better decisions regarding my abusers. I continued instead to remain in a spiraling cycle. My lessons were yet to be learned.

If I told my parents and they didn't call the proper authorities; then at least I had the right to call the authorities myself. If nothing was

∞

done through the proper authorities, then I at least had done my job. When I do my job, I perform my purpose. There are a lot of silent voices in the world, and sadly, many of them are children, like I was. Abusers have to be exposed if they are to be stopped. When the truth stops being exposed past your parents, they have just prevented the exposure and the chance for the abuse to stop beyond you. For people who are abused, it is important to understand that the cycle will continue possibly towards others you may know and love if the abuser isn't stopped. You can't care about the abuser more than you love yourself and a world full of other innocent victims.

Abuse doesn't start or stop with me; it starts or stops with the abuser. We have to do something about the abuser. I didn't understand exactly at what point in the book I would come to an understanding about my abuse, but in reality, in the seventh grade, I didn't have a clue. The lessons still continued.

I may be experienced to speak on the topic of sexual predators now, but before I became the teacher, I definitely had to learn it first, which means I had to experience it first. Only students can become teachers. I had to learn some even harder lessons, but I'm thankful to be able to help someone else to heal before their cycle continues. Now the journey becomes tougher.

∞

In chapter thirteen, volume one entitled, "The Whippings," Mother Jordon was a very loving leader. She taught what she believed to be right. She led according to what she felt God was showing her. I understand that we are all human and no one is perfect therefore, I don't criticize her for teaching what she believed, even in instances where I may have been confused. When I recalled this memory recently with my mother, she told me that she remembered this incident happening and Bishop Nichols confessing and apologizing over the pulpit for whipping one of his children in anger and vowing to never whip his children in anger again. Bishop Nichols had to understand that the exposure of shameful things is designed to move us to change and grow and I celebrate his growth because he is an awesome father, husband, and pastor today. He has been a wonderful mentor to me and is a walking testament of faith. Everytime I talk to him, I am amazed at just how real God is. I love him and Sister Nichols for the loving people of God they are today.

The most powerful thing any great leader must realize is that we are all vulnerable because no one is perfect. We shouldn't look for any perfect beings. There is only a perfect God. I looked upon Mother Jordon as a perfect being who couldn't teach me wrong. God never intends for a human being to be your total source. Each being has within them power to seek wisdom from God personally. Whenever a word or prophecy was spoken, no matter how confusing, I believed with my whole heart God spoke through my leaders to me. This is not to say that my leader wasn't a woman of God; this is to say that I was also a young woman of God who just didn't know how to tap into God in a personal way that enabled me to know what God had planned for my life. I only knew how to be led by people and because people are not perfect, it is so important to know how to hear from a perfect God who often speaks to your thoughts and gives you wisdom from within. I just didn't know how to tap into the God within me so I went about my life trusting blindly in people. God often works through people, but you have to be careful to ensure that

∞

people are not your total source. Your main source should be God, so I would encourage everyone to spend some time and ask God to give you understanding and an ability to hear personally from him and then spend some quiet time listening to your thoughts as he speaks to you. You will know it is God because your thoughts will enlighten you as you discover defining moments in your life. I spend more time listening than I spend talking when I go to God in prayer. And for me, this helps me to find more purpose from day to day regarding myself and what I need to focus on becoming. I'm always working towards a higher mark because I can see that I am destined for more than where I presently am in life. I have absolutely all the respect in the world for the spiritual leaders who God placed in my life and I am so thankful to God for covering me during the times I didn't know him personally. It is necessary for me to be covered, so I thank God for the church family who loved and covered me.

Now I look for God to lead me and speak to me daily in my quiet moments of meditation. Most of what I hear from the Pastor at the church I currently attend is a confirmation of what has already been shown to me. Everything I hear from the people of God who have been placed in my life adds to my growth. I'm moving forward. Even more important though; when I talk to my past church leaders, I am amazed and blessed by their testimonies of faith because they prove to me just how real God is. I don't think God would be so evident to me if I didn't know him personally. I know God lives in them and I can recognize the spirit of God in his people when I'm in their presence, no matter who they are.

Because I have a strong personal relationship with God now, he places both old and new leaders in my life who speak words which line up with God's purpose for my life. My ability to go directly to God and rely on him to be my source is the key to my ability to walk in destiny and purpose because this allows me to be more in touch with my inner self. To truly know God, is to know one's self. Godly assur-

∞

ance is connected to self-assurance.

God knew me before I was formed in my mother's womb and he called me here with a divine purpose and destiny. *How am I to know my divine purpose and destiny without personally hearing from God?* It takes daily meditation, and quiet time alone listening to the inner voice inside you to hear God speaking. It also takes a willingness to do some soul searching. You have to seek out answers to help you get through the process of life's journey.

When I find myself going through challenges, I ask God to show me what I need to learn in order to overcome the challenge. I calmly go through the process knowing it's only a temporary situation as long as I learn what changes are needed in order to overcome it.

No matter how much I cried out, moaned, fasted and stayed on my knees praying, I always waited on a word from Mother Jordon to be the direct voice of God in my life because I didn't have a personal relationship with him. Many interpretations, prophecies, correction and direction came from Mother Jordon's mouth. I depended on her to tell me who I was, where I was going, and what God was speaking to me. I'm not pointing this out to say that Mother Jordon wasn't a great leader. I am simply saying the word of God would have been more effective to me if I had a personal relationship with God in addition to being led by my leaders. There were other ordained prophets in the church and I believed them because I believed Mother Jordon who called them prophets; not because I truly knew God, even though I had accepted God in my heart and believed he was real. There is a big difference in believing and accepting God's spirit in your heart and having a deep personal relationship with him. People ask me, *"how do you know God is real?"* It's not really something I can show them because it is a very personal experience and belief. You have to test the waters for yourself and know and believe him for yourself.

∞

I don't want to jump ahead. It will be well into my adult life when I learn lessons I speak about in the above mentioned paragraphs. What you are witnessing is regression leading to progression many years later as I examine all the things in my life. I am enjoying the process of memories as I celebrate growth today.

∞

In volume one, chapter fourteen entitled "Strict," *what was going on with the relationship between me and Daddy? Why couldn't he just talk to me and why didn't he trust me?* As I look back, I'm realizing I even had a problem with sitting in Daddy's lap growing up. I didn't want to be babied up, the way he loved on my sister Sonia. Sonia was always hugging and kissing Daddy and tickling him and lying on his belly and Daddy was treating her like a little baby all the time. I hated the thought of being treated like a baby. I could never sleep with Mama and Daddy the way Sonia was always sleeping with them at night. Mama had to make her sleep in her own bed a lot of nights. She always acted like a baby. I never lay on Daddy's belly and I tried to make our goodnight kisses quick every night. It was like something I had to get over with so I could be done with the uncomfortable feeling of having to kiss him on the lips. Kissing was still embarrassing to me. Saying I love you wasn't hard because I loved Daddy no matter what.

On the one hand, I was carrying scars from Granddaddy. I just didn't realize it. On the other hand, Daddy's controlling behavior was way beyond normal. This was extreme behavior to control me and keep me from boys. Daddy showed too much mistrust and was becoming too possessive, especially once it got to the point I couldn't let a boy touch me.

Daddy felt the need to always watch me like a hawk, to the point of keeping me on the porch. Yes, something was very wrong here. I felt like he was punishing me for having a neat figure which made me wish I was skinny more and more. People were always commenting about my figure and warning Daddy to watch me with my neat figure both at church and at home. Pastor Nichols was even looking at me with a condemning eye. I often felt inadequate around him like Pastor Nichols believed I was fast or something. I knew he was saying little things to Daddy warning him to watch me.

∞

As children growing up, our perceptions can be distorted when it comes to how we assess our friendships. The girls that I hung out with in my neighborhood could have just as easily felt that I was a "goodie two shoes." They may have even felt that I was jealous of them the same way I felt they were envious and bitter towards me. I was young and still learning about life and so were the girls I bonded with growing up. I isolated myself as a result of my daddy's controlling behavior. I never confided in them about why I was isolating myself, so they could very easily express a completely different viewpoint of our friendship. As children we all struggle to understand our lives that are filled with a mixture of our individual issues. I'm sure we were all dealing with some things. I realize now that as young girls growing up together, we all have had to face pain and we've all had times when we may have been misunderstood. In friendships, some bonds are stronger than others; nevertheless, there is an ever-lasting bond in my heart especially with Paulina and Anita that will never end. I originally wrote this chapter about ten years ago. I was in a place of pain. My view of my youth has changed significantly but I still felt it was necessary to show the painful side of myself because so many people today are in painful spaces in their lives. Reaching out to those that have been wounded in life is my inspiration for writing my memoirs.

∞

In volume one, chapter fifteen entitled, "The Boys," I realize now I had a problem with guys controlling me and it possibly started with Granddaddy, who I was determined wouldn't control me, even if I had to lay there with my Grandmother all night and starve. Then again, Pastor Jacobs made me feel defenseless to protect myself as well, even though I wanted to stand up to him.

A lot was happening with my relationship with the males in my house. I kept my distance from Scootie in public because he seemed to want to control me. He was too overprotective. He came to my defense even when I felt it wasn't necessary.

I had to find a way to gain control of my life. It was slipping away from me into Daddy's and Scootie's hands. Guys were destroying my freedom. I may as well have been promiscuous if I had to be punished and locked away. I felt like I was in prison. I couldn't do anything. I couldn't go anywhere. I still didn't want Granddaddy to win either. If I gave in to guys sexually, I felt like Granddaddy, Pastor Jacobs, and every other guy, would gain control over me. In my mind that meant that I would be defeated. I thought that they would win and I would fail if I ever had sex with a guy.

This attitude carried over in many ways towards me making sure I placed certain boundaries on how intimate I would allow a guy to be with me. With Murphy, John, Mark, and Vance, there was a definite cut off point for me, and sexual intercourse was not even conceivable in my mind. I had already told myself, not until marriage which I hoped was a long way ahead of me, and I knew I wouldn't be marrying any of these guys.

∞

In volume one, chapter seventeen entitled "Why Me," at that age, I only asked, "*Why me?*" Now I examine all the repetitive things which seem to be pattern forming in my past and present simply because there is a lesson to be learned in order for the cycle to be broken. Why God chose me, is not the question I need to ask. I needed to focus on how to turn my negative experiences into the blessings that they were really intended to become.

When I had Murphy paying for all the junk food from the candy lady, I didn't realize how dangerous this kind of game was. Murphy probably wanted to pay me back for some time. Gregory thought up a way for Murphy to even the score and they both showed me what happens when girls play dangerous games with guys. Gregory had it in for my type due to his pent-up anger and aggression. I could have been any girl, but Gregory was looking to get even with the world. Murphy gave him a reason to come after me. I didn't understand at my age what was going on and why. I'm glad that I can look back at an incident that had an impact on me. It resulted in a lesson learned and now I can share it with others.

When you can heal, then you can become the healer of many. Instead of questioning life, and all that happens in it, I now embrace life, and all that happens in it. I smile when I reflect back on my life now because, I can write this book and I can tell this story because of my life. I can study my life and pull so much out of it now. Every time I reflect on my pain, I do not focus on the pain, but the healing powers that come as a result of my willingness to face my pain, feel my pain and speak about my pain. Pain is a part of life. My job is not to be afraid of this, but rather, to accept it and find the good behind the pain. Whenever I can get to the point where I can see the good and the blessings, I can find strength. Everything that happens in life has a reason. It's not about good or bad, right or wrong. It's about choices, consequences and lessons.

∞

As a result of my choices in every situation in my life, consequences resulted. The ramifications of the poor choices I made resulted in unhealthy circumstances, instead of the change I was seeking. I simply needed to learn from the lesson and begin to make better decisions so that I could experience a positive change. Even though I wasn't at fault for what happened and I couldn't control what was going on, Murphy was paying me back in a sense for playing games with him. I know now those kinds of games are dangerous. Change in this definition and for this purpose, is simply an indication of maturity and growth.

I put on my tough skin as I went through this journey of life. I seldom cried during this time because tears represented defeat in my mind. If anyone defeated me, they had to pay a price for the pain they caused me. I learned to punish others by blocking them out of my life. If I cut them off, and made them invisible, I eventually witnessed a longing for them to be seen and heard by me. Everyone wants to matter. If I made them insignificant, they hurt worse than they hurt me to begin with. Pastor Jacobs showed me this a long time ago. This message grew stronger over the years. It eventually became my greatest tool. At the same time, it was my handicap. My long journey continues.

∞

In volume one, chapter eighteen entitled "Deja Vu," what I didn't understand about Ralph was he was behaving like the typical rapist. Rape is an act of aggression and is one of the most violent and dehumanizing forms of human abuse. A rapist may sexually assault any woman regardless of age, appearance, social status, or race. Motivation for rape is aggression, domination, and power. Rapists want you to submit to their authority. They want total control. In my confused state and with my limited knowledge, I was beginning to think I was being targeted because of my figure. Ralph most likely targeted me more because he wanted to dominate someone who didn't appear easy to succumb to being seduced. I was always saying no to boys about sex. Growing up with Ralph, there had been times when I punched him for touching me telling him to keep his hands off me and many other times when he saw me confronting other boys. He was one of the boys who played football with me and saw me walk off the field over an inappropriate touch. Rapists want to dominate and attain power over their victims, so he was proving to me he was the one with the power. My crying and pleading fueled his desires to continue. Ralph would later end up in jail serving a long sentence for rape and drugs. He had also beaten and choked his other victim. He needed to be stopped early on. As a child at my level of understanding, I didn't really understand how to deal with this kind of situation. Dealing with this situation properly would have simply meant I would have reported him to the police.

By this time, I'm convinced boys only wanted one thing and one thing only from me. The only reason a guy even looked at me was because he liked my body. I was also convinced I must not be very pretty since I never heard boys calling me beautiful. Instead of treating me with respect they only talked about my body. In my mind, Ralph would not have been so cruel if I was pretty. A lot of girls I knew were called pretty and beautiful even though they didn't have a figure quite as defined as mine with my extra curvy hips and butt. I'd rather be thought of as pretty. I hated knowing a boy was only

∞

interested in my body.

I went back through a mixture of events in my life in order to heal. I'm able to look back at all the choices I made and all the many paths I had to explore. I understand there is a positive purpose for everything in my life. I can only teach what I need to learn. I'm telling my story as I represent the proud African American Woman I am, in order to heal a nation.

I grew up in a black "Holiness" church most of my life. While being brought up in this church, I was programmed to believe if you don't live inside of this "Holiness" box with all the beliefs being taught inside of it, you will go to hell. As children growing up in this church, we kept each other's secrets of incest, rape, physical abuse, and pedophilia activities committed by family and some of the church leaders. The solution to every problem was always the same; hours of moaning, praying, fasting and crying on bended knees day after day waiting for God to come down and fix everything. I found myself wondering a lot, *where is God? Does he hear us down here begging for help? Why hasn't he fixed it? Are we not worthy? What are we doing wrong?*

After attending several churches, my eyes were open to the fact that there is too much confusion with respect to religion. There's a fine line between serving God and being controlled by religious traditions. When you're hurting and running to the church looking for answers, sometimes it's hard to understand the difference. Church can be a strong source of strength; therefore it has become a dependent resource in the lives of millions. Unfortunately, not every church is flourishing. If the church isn't flourishing, there's an inability to grow. Not every church leader has the capacity to deal with serious issues in a practical way, so people perish for lack of knowledge. A church is only as strong and wise as its leaders. I mean no condemnation because as I have said before, I have great respect for

∞

the people of God. However, my mind has been opened up and God has allowed me to step out of the small box I was living inside of in order to grow me and take me to new levels beyond where I was in my limited mind. I had to come out of self condemnation and learn to see myself as God sees me. I realized that God says all good things about me and I didn't realize this until I listened to myself saying bad things. I realized God doesn't speak that way about me. He would never have put me down the way I was always putting myself down. God is all positive, all seeing, and all knowing and he loves me no matter what. When I say I can't make it, he says I can. When I say I'm a failure, he says I'm a success. There was a time when someone called me profane names, I didn't get offended. I simply looked at them and said, it doesn't matter what you call me, it doesn't make me what you call me. I am who God says I am and he doesn't say I'm any of those things nor does he say that about you. Just because you say it doesn't make me those things. The more I opened up my mind, the more I began to reject negativity and accept positivity, so even in the midst of trouble, I see good things coming.

My story is a testimony for people who find themselves at a standstill spiritually. God is so much bigger than denominations, traditions, and religious interpretations of the bible that differ from church to church. I had given up on church for many years until one day I learned to listen to my inner voice at home all alone in my room. That inner voice is God leading, teaching, and loving me. The more I grow to understand the inner voice, the more I know who I am. Knowing God means knowing what's right for me, including the church to attend. Let me reiterate, I respect and appreciate every spiritual leader past and present who has ever been placed in my life and am thankful that God was keeping me covered by the many prayers of my spiritual leaders. I have no doubt God lives in them all. I love them all and have learned so many things about God, faith, and prayer. As a result of being raised in the church, so much good has been

∞

deposited in me in spite of my pain and I have been truly blessed. I take nothing negative out of my church upbringing because everything has worked for my good. God took me to a different place in order to open up my mind and understand my true purpose and my true journey. God is not surprised, nor is he confused about all the churches and denominations that exist in this world today. In every church you can find something different about the interpretations of the bible and God is not even surprised by this. There is so much we can pull from one another because every Christian oriented church believes God is a healer, deliverer, and problem solver, and he deserves praise, honor, and glory. We all know that God is good and most importantly, we all have faith. These beliefs allow God to see one body of believers instead of denominations and traditions that vary from church to church. I have to truly know God to be led by God and I have to believe wherever he leads me will transcend every wall I have lived inside of that has limited me and held me back. When I was finally open to explore other churches, I witnessed God's power and recognized that his spirit was just as much in the words of the ministers I was seeing and hearing as they were in the leaders I had known and grown comfortable with all my life. I realized truth was in their ministry as I witnessed strong revelations and demonstrations of God in awesome and new ways. I went to God and asked him if I was going to lose my soul for leaving the teachings and traditions of the church where I was taught to strongly believe that any other church or any other way of teaching would cause me to miss out and be turned away from God. God spoke to me plainly and said, "I am bigger than a church and I am so much greater than religion. If, and only if you are willing to open your mind up, will you understand what these words mean. I realized that religion is often defined within boundaries and limitations that keep you from growing outside of the church you belong to. It often separates you from other churches and people of God, so when God said to me that I am greater than religion, he was simply saying my soul salvation wasn't dependent upon me belonging to a particular church group. God is global and he transcends space. He is everywhere. I just needed to have an open mind to be able to experience him outside the boundaries of the small space I thought I had to remain in, in order to be saved and make it into heaven. I had to learn to have an open mind to receive new instructions and to grow and learn more than what I know up to this point. That open mind has taken me outside of the box and I am finding God can do above and beyond all that I can think and/or imagine. At the same time, I honor the church I was raised in and I understand that everything they teach honors God as well. When God was taking me to a different place, it wasn't about right or wrong teachings; it was just my time to allow God to take me where he could begin to do the work in my life that lined up with my purpose and destiny. Instead of being confused during my time of exploring and questioning varying beliefs, and interpretations, and expanding my knowledge of the word, I began to understand just how similar people of God are in the belief that God is the answer to everything. I'm grateful to God for opening up my understanding. I'm even more thankful to God for giving me the courage to tell my story.

I want every victim of abuse to understand they have absolutely nothing to be ashamed of and nothing to hide. I've been in my sick bed too long. It's now time to rise up, be healed and go out and heal a nation.

I did change all the names to protect those still struggling with the fear of exposure for whatever reasons. I have a duty to respect the right to allow others to heal in their own time and in their own way without judgment or criticism. I'm not God.

There is the very real exposure of the black Holiness church that I grew up in. My family and friends, whom I love are members of this church.

∞

I made the decision to tell my story because my life and my family's life are not in vain.

I made this choice because someone may be helped by my story. I'm so thankful for my husband and my daughter who have allowed me to expose so much about our lives. Our true source of power is in both knowing and understanding our history.

I had no idea how far and how detailed this journey would lead me but three volumes later, I thank God I made it so far.

∞

_____'s Healing Roads Journal

_____

_____

_____

_____

_____

_____

_____

_____

_____

_____

_____

_____

∞

∞

∞

$$\infty$$

∞

$$\underline{\infty}$$

Find out why Tweety's nightmares seemed
to be real in

"Don't Touch Me"
Volume II

What lessons will Tweety learn in

"The Healing Roads"
Volume II

The Journey Continues....

www.ingramcontent.com/pod-product-compliance
Lightning Source LLC
Chambersburg PA
CBHW060721030426
42337CB00017B/2951